火车站

How We Organize Ourselves | Non-Fiction Series

Copyright © 2022 by Level Learning, INC. and Washington Yu Ying PCS™
Original and Edited Text Copyright © 2022 by Washington Yu Ying PCS™

All rights reserved. No part of this book in whole or part may be reproduced without written permission from the publisher.

Published by Level Learning, INC.

Content Contributors:
Washington Yu Ying PCS™ - Qianyi (Shirley) Zhang, Pearl Zao He You
Level Learning - Jingyao Qi

Illustrations by: Josh Taira

Leveling classification based on Level Learning standard.
For full description, visit www.levellearning.com

ISBN 978-1-64040-110-5
Simplified Chinese Edition

About Level Learning:
Level Learning provides a literacy focused curriculum specifically designed for K-12 Chinese as a Second Language classrooms. Our program offers 20 levels of specific and detailed objectives, leveled texts and passages, mastery-based online assessment, and analytics to enable data-driven instruction. Level Learning reading curriculum for both literature and informational text emphasize grammar and comprehension skills to help teachers develop confident and independent Chinese language readers. The non-fiction series of books are specifically designed to support our informational text course based on multiple national standards. To learn more about our entire offering, visit www.levellearning.com.

About Washington Yu Ying PCS™:
Washington Yu Ying PCS is a Mandarin English dual language immersion International Baccalaureate (IB) World school. Yu Ying's mission is to inspire and prepare young people to create a better world by challenging them to reach their full potential in a nurturing Chinese/English educational environment. Yu Ying's comprehensive IB, dual immersion curriculum equips students with global competencies for success in the real world. As a leader in immersion education, Yu Ying is determined to advance Chinese language programs and global citizenry education by helping other schools create and strengthen their Chinese programs. For more information, email: products@washingtonyuying.org

你去过火车站吗？

火车站有售票处。

人们在售票处买火车票。

火车站有候车室。

人们在候车室等火车。

火车站有站台。

人们在站台上火车和下火车。

火车站里有很多人。

人们拿着行李。

人们拿着车票。

人们要去哪里呢?

人们坐火车去工作。

人们坐火车去旅行。

这边和那边是反方向。

不要坐错车呀!

Glossary

	Pinyin	English Definition
火车	huǒ chē	train
站	zhàn	station
售票处	shòu piào chù	ticket office
买	mǎi	to buy
票	piào	ticket
候车室	hòu chē shì	waiting room
等	děng	to wait
站台	zhàn tái	platform
很多	hěn duō	a lot
拿	ná	to hold
行李	xíng li	luggage
工作	gōng zuò	work
旅行	lǚ xíng	vacation
边	biān	side
反方向	fǎn fāng xiàng	opposite direction
错	cuò	wrong

www.ingramcontent.com/pod-product-compliance
Lightning Source LLC
Chambersburg PA
CBHW041226070526
44584CB00001B/110